Cuteep Photoees
Xmas 2013
XO

Happiness

Family

Gr...

Purpose

D1122953

THE BEST *things* IN *Life* AREN'T THINGS

10 ESSENTIALS FOR A MEANINGFUL LIFE

Peggy Anderson

Dedicated with endless love
to my parents

MARY AND RICHARD CRISORIO

TABLE OF *Contents*

"EVERYTHING THAT'S
REALLY WORTHWHILE
IN LIFE COMES TO
US FREE—OUR MINDS,
OUR SOULS, OUR BODIES,
OUR HOPES, OUR DREAMS,
OUR INTELLIGENCE, OUR
LOVE OF FAMILY AND
FRIENDS AND COUNTRY.
ALL OF THESE PRICELESS
POSSESSIONS ARE FREE."

~EARL NIGHTINGALE

INTRODUCTION

IN THE CHAOS of everyday life, we often find ourselves spending *most* of our time on things that matter *least*. At the end of our lives, what our bank account was, the type of house we lived in, or the kind of car we drove will not be important…but the world may be different because of the core values we held true.

There are numerous distractions along the road of life that can sidetrack us. Sometimes difficult choices need to be made. However, if we have to sacrifice material possessions for values, we have made the right choice.

Our lives become meaningful when we focus on those essentials that enrich the lives of others…and in return, enrich our own lives, essential values like:

gratitude, character, kindness, faith, love, courage, family, friendship, happiness and purpose.

The words in this book celebrate and reinforce these core values. It is my hope that they will help you remember—

the best things in life aren't things at all.

GRATITUDE

"Gratitude is not only the greatest of virtues, but the parent of all others."

MARCUS TULLIUS CICERO

"GRATITUDE UNLOCKS THE *fullness of life. It turns what we have into enough, and more. It turns denial into acceptance, chaos to order, confusion to clarity. It can turn a meal into a feast, a house into a home, a stranger into a friend. Gratitude makes sense of our past, brings peace for today, and creates a vision for tomorrow." – Melody Beattie*

An anonymous author said:

"Be thankful that you don't already have everything you desire. If you did, what would there be to look forward to? Be thankful when you don't know something for it gives you the opportunity to learn. Be thankful for difficult times. During those times, we grow. Be thankful for limitations; because they give opportunities for improvement. Be thankful for each new challenge because it will build strength and character. Be thankful for mistakes. They teach us valuable lessons. It is easy to be thankful for the good things. A life of rich fulfillment comes to those who are thankful for the setbacks.

"Gratitude can turn a negative into a positive. Find a way to be thankful for your troubles and they can become your blessings."

Two of the most significant words are "thank you." These simple words express our appreciation to others. They convey gratitude for kindness that has been shown to us. These two simple words can have a powerful and positive ripple effect.

*A*t times, our own light goes out and is rekindled
by a spark from another person. Each of us has cause
to think with deep gratitude of those who have
lighted the flame within us.

ALBERT SCHWEITZER

PRAISE THE BRIDGE THAT CARRIED YOU OVER.

GEORGE COLMAN

*H*e is a wise man who does not grieve for things which
he has not, but rejoices for those which he has.

EPICTETUS

GRATITUDE IS THE FAIREST BLOSSOM
WHICH SPRINGS FROM THE SOUL.

HENRY WARD BEECHER

*P*eople who live the most fulfilling lives are the ones
who are always rejoicing at what they have.

RICHARD CARLSON

BE THANKFUL FOR WHAT YOU HAVE;
YOU WILL END UP HAVING MORE.

OPRAH WINFREY

*Y*ou won't be happy with more until
you're happy with what you've got.

VIKI KING

FEELING GRATITUDE AND NOT EXPRESSING IT IS
LIKE WRAPPING A PRESENT AND NOT GIVING IT.

WILLIAM ARTHUR WARD

*L*et us be grateful to the people who make us happy;
they are the charming gardeners who
make our souls blossom.

MARCEL PROUST

*D*evelop an attitude of gratitude, and give thanks for
everything that happens to you, knowing that every step
forward is a step toward achieving something bigger
and better than your current situation.

BRIAN TRACY

GRATITUDE IS WHEN MEMORY IS STORED
IN THE HEART AND NOT IN THE MIND.

LIONEL HAMPTON

*W*hen you arise in the morning, think of what a precious
privilege it is to be alive—to breathe, to think, to enjoy,
to love—then make the day count.

STEVE MARABOLI

WE CAN ONLY BE SAID TO BE ALIVE
IN THOSE MOMENTS WHEN OUR HEARTS
ARE CONSCIOUS OF OUR TREASURES.

THORTON WILDER

*W*hen we choose not to focus on what is missing from our
lives but are grateful for the abundance that's present…
we experience heaven on earth.

SARAH BAN BREATHNACH

When it comes to life,
the critical thing is whether you
take things for granted or
take them with gratitude.

GILBERT KEITH CHESTERTON

GRAT

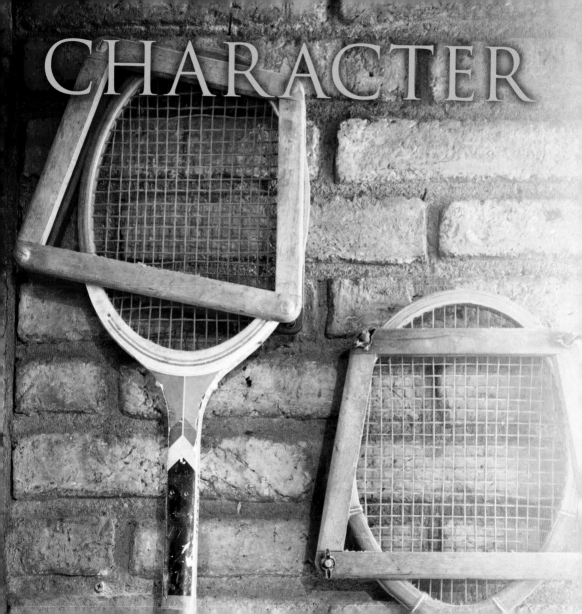

CHARACTER

"The character that takes command in moments of crucial choices has already been determined by … the little choices of years past—by all those times when the voice of conscience was at war with the voice of temptation, whispering the lie that 'it really doesn't matter.'"

———— • ◆ • ————

THIS STORY BY author Bob Kelly shows that the most important person you need to face every day…is you!

In the world of tennis, Eliot Teltscher never became as famous as Jimmy Connors or John McEnroe. Yet, during his professional career, from 1977 to 1988, he was consistently ranked among the world's Top-10 players, winning 10 singles titles and more than $1.6 million in prize money.

Teltscher began playing tennis at age nine. After high school, he received a tennis scholarship to UCLA, and was named an All-American as a freshman. He left college to turn professional. In 1982, he was ranked #6 in the world. He retired as a player in 1988, and currently serves as a National Coach for the United States Tennis Association.

Despite his many accomplishments, when asked about the highlights of his career, the first thing he usually mentions isn't about victories or awards. Instead, he describes a match he lost, but which speaks volumes about him.

In January 1982, playing Vitas Gerulaitis, also a Top-10 player, the latter was at match point in the final set. His last shot barely cleared the net, seemingly out of Teltscher's reach but, somehow, he got his racket on the ball and lofted it over his opponent's head, winning the point.

There was a problem, however, which neither Gerulaitis nor the umpire, nor anyone else realized. But Teltscher did—and nothing else mattered. In rushing for that final shot, his racket barely grazed the net, which violated the rules. Without hesitation, he informed the umpire, costing him the point and the match.

B.C. Forbes, who founded Forbes *magazine nearly a century ago, once commented, "Integrity is the basis of all true-blue success." For Eliot Teltscher, he faced a moment when his integrity and his character were at stake, and that was far more important than winning a tennis match. In defeat, he achieved not only a real victory but "true-blue success."*

CHARACTER IS
MUCH EASIER KEPT THAN RECOVERED.

THOMAS PAINE

*O*ur character is what we do
when we think no one is looking.

H. JACKSON BROWN JR.

INTEGRITY IS THE ESSENCE OF
EVERYTHING SUCCESSFUL.

R. BUCKMINSTER FULLER

NEVER SEPARATE THE LIFE YOU LEAD
FROM THE WORDS YOU SPEAK.

PAUL WELLSTONE

Character—the willingness to accept responsibility
for one's own life—is the source from
which self-respect springs.

JOAN DIDION

TRY NOT TO BECOME A MAN OF SUCCESS, BUT
RATHER TRY TO BECOME A MAN OF VALUE.

ALBERT EINSTEIN

A quiet conscience sleeps in thunder.

ENGLISH PROVERB

ADVERSITY DOESN'T BUILD CHARACTER, IT REVEALS IT.

UNKNOWN

*C*haracter is like a tree and reputation like its shadow.
The shadow is what we think of it; the tree is the real thing.

ABRAHAM LINCOLN

*T*he ultimate measure of a man is not where he stands
in moments of comfort and convenience, but where
he stands at times of challenge and controversy.

DR. MARTIN LUTHER KING JR.

IT IS OUR CHARACTER THAT SUPPORTS
THE PROMISE OF OUR FUTURE...

WILLIAM J. BENNETT

*W*hat lies behind us and what lies before us are
small matters compared to what lies within us.

RALPH WALDO EMERSON

Character

FAME IS A VAPOR, POPULARITY AN ACCIDENT,
AND RICHES TAKE WINGS. ONLY ONE THING
ENDURES AND THAT IS CHARACTER.

HORACE GREELEY

*C*haracter cannot be developed in ease and quiet.
Only through experience of trial and suffering
can the soul be strengthened, vision cleared,
ambition inspired and success achieved.

HELEN KELLER

EXAMPLE IS NOT THE MAIN THING IN
INFLUENCING OTHERS. IT IS THE ONLY THING.

ALBERT SCHWEITZER

I hope I shall always possess firmness and virtue enough to maintain what I consider the most enviable of all titles, the character of an honest man.

GEORGE WASHINGTON

A HEART NEEDS ONLY ITS OWN VOICE
TO DO WHAT IS RIGHT.

VANNA BONTA

*H*ave the courage to say no. Have the courage to face the truth. Do the right thing because it is right. These are the magic keys to living your life with integrity.

W. CLEMENT STONE

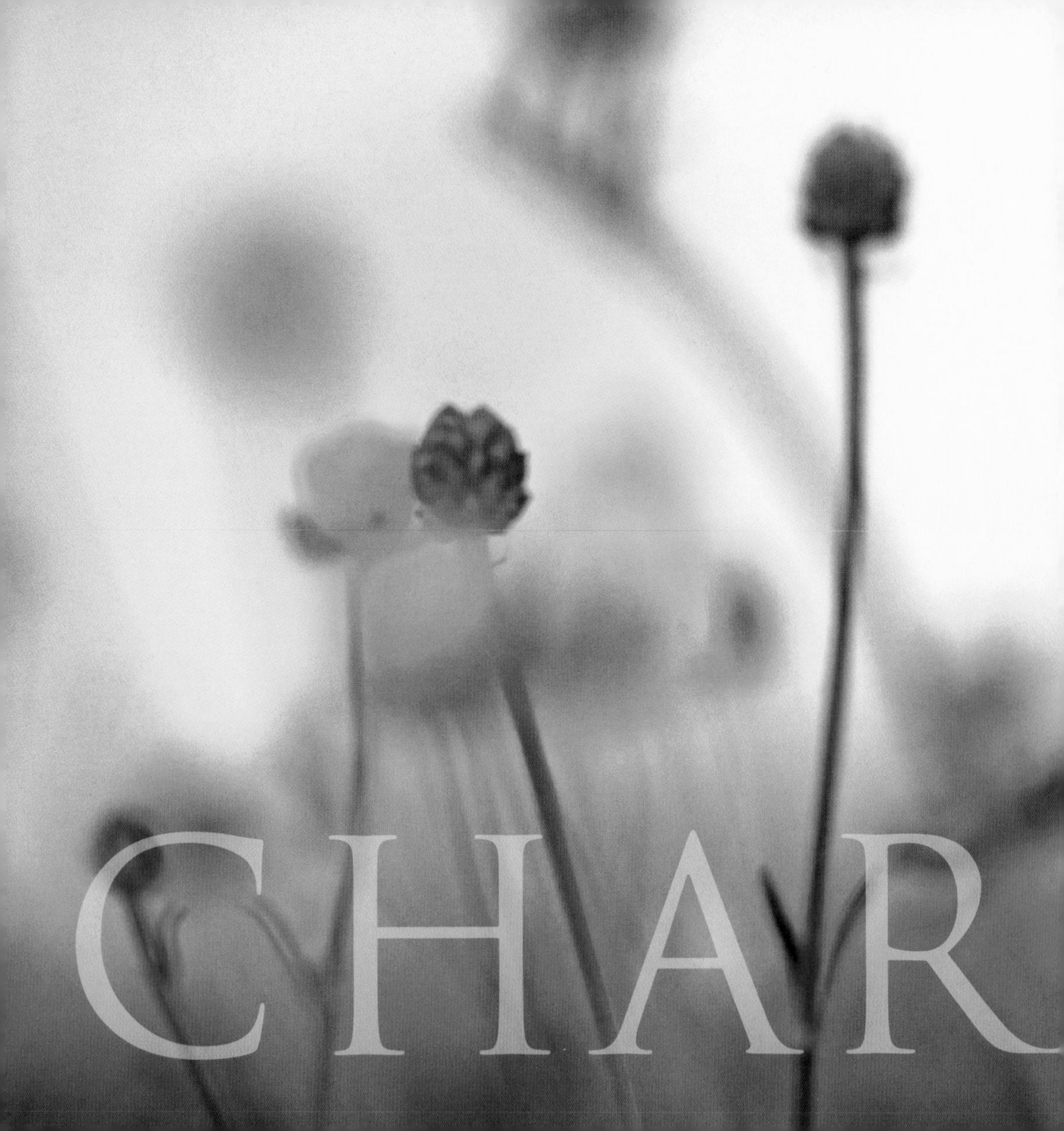
CHAR

THE BEST INDEX TO A PERSON'S
CHARACTER IS HOW HE TREATS PEOPLE
WHO CAN'T DO HIM ANY GOOD...

ABIGAIL VAN BUREN

KINDNESS

> *"Kindness is a language which the deaf can
> hear and the blind can see."*
>
> MARK TWAIN

———— • ◆ • ————

WHEN ALDOUS HUXLEY, the great English writer and pioneer in the study of techniques to develop human potential, was asked about the most effective technique for transforming a person's life, he simply replied,

> *"It's a little embarrassing that after years and years of research,
> my best answer is—just be a little kinder."*

That's the paradox of kindness. It doesn't feel powerful at all. In fact, it almost feels too simple to be important. But, as Huxley said, it is the #1 thing that can transform your life…and the lives of those around you. This story brings the power of kindness to life better than any I've heard:

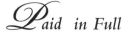 *aid in Full*

One day, a poor boy who was selling goods from door-to-door to pay his way through school, found he had only one thin dime left, and he was hungry. He decided he would ask for a meal at the next house. However, he lost his nerve when a lovely young woman opened the door.

Instead of a meal, he asked for a drink of water. She thought he looked hungry and so she brought him a large glass of milk. He drank it slowly, and then asked, "How much do I owe you?"

"You don't owe me anything," she replied. "Mother has taught us never to accept pay for a kindness." He said, "Then I thank you from my heart." As Howard Kelly left that house, he not only felt stronger physically, but his faith in God and man was strengthened also. He had been ready to give up and quit.

Years later, that young woman became critically ill. The local doctors were baffled. They finally sent her to the big city, where they called in specialists to study her rare disease.

Dr. Howard Kelly was called in for the consultation. When he heard the name of the town she came from, he went down the hall of the hospital to her room. Dressed in his doctor's gown, he went in to see her. He recognized her at once. He went back to the consultation room determined to do his best to save her life. From that day, he gave special attention to the case.

After a long struggle, the battle was won. Dr. Kelly requested the business office to pass the final billing to him for approval. He looked at it, then wrote something on the edge, and the bill was sent to her room. She feared to open it, for she was sure it would take the rest of her life to pay for it all. Finally, she looked, and something caught her attention on the side of the bill. She read these words:

"Paid in full with one glass of milk…"

Signed

Dr. Howard Kelly

Dr. Howard Kelly was a distinguished physician who, in 1895, founded the Johns Hopkins Division of Gynecologic Oncology at Johns Hopkins University. According to Dr. Kelly's biographer, Audrey Davis, the doctor was on a walking trip through Northern Pennsylvania one spring day when he stopped by a farm house for a drink of water.

Kindness

I expect to pass through this world but once;
any good thing therefore that I can do, or any kindness
that I can show to any fellow creature, let me not defer
or neglect it, for I shall not pass this way again.

WILLIAM PENN

A WARM SMILE IS THE UNIVERSAL
LANGUAGE OF KINDNESS.

WILLIAM ARTHUR WARD

*Y*ou cannot do a kindness too soon, for you never know
how soon it will be too late.

RALPH WALDO EMERSON

NEVER LOOK DOWN ON ANYBODY,
UNLESS YOU'RE HELPING THEM UP.

JESSE JACKSON SR.

*K*ind words can be short and easy to speak,
but their echoes are truly endless.

MOTHER TERESA

NO ONE HAS EVER BECOME POOR BY GIVING.

ANNE FRANK

FOR IT IS IN GIVING THAT WE RECEIVE.

SAINT FRANCIS OF ASSISI

*T*oday, give a stranger one of your smiles.
It might be the only sunshine he sees all day.

H. JACKSON BROWN JR.

AS WE WORK TO CREATE LIGHT FOR OTHERS, WE NATURALLY LIGHT OUR OWN WAY.

MARY ANNE RADMACHER

*T*hose who bring sunshine into the lives of others
cannot keep it from themselves.

JAMES M. BARRIE

———•◆•———

A BIT OF FRAGRANCE ALWAYS CLINGS
TO THE HAND THAT GIVES ROSES.

CHINESE PROVERB

*T*he smallest act of kindness is worth
more than the grandest intention.

OSCAR WILDE

NEVER LOSE A CHANCE OF
SAYING A KIND WORD.

WILLIAM MAKEPEACE THACKERAY

*Y*ou can't live a perfect day without doing something for
someone who will never be able to repay you.

JOHN WOODEN

I don't want my life to be defined by what is etched on a tombstone. I want it to be defined in what is etched in the lives and hearts of those I've touched.

STEVE MARABOLI

YOU WILL RISE BY LIFTING OTHERS.

ROBERT G. INGERSOLL

G reat acts of love are done by those who are habitually performing small acts of kindness.

VICTOR HUGO

KIND

*T*OO OFTEN WE UNDERESTIMATE THE POWER
OF A TOUCH, A SMILE, A KIND WORD, A LISTENING EAR,
AN HONEST COMPLIMENT, OR THE SMALLEST ACT OF CARING,
ALL OF WHICH HAVE THE POTENTIAL TO TURN A LIFE AROUND.

LEO F. BUSCAGLIA

NESS

FAITH

"Faith consists in believing when it is beyond the power of reason to believe."

VOLTAIRE

FOR MORE THAN 100 years, runners tried to break the four-minute mile. It was considered the "Holy Grail" of track and field. Many said it couldn't be done. In fact, doctors wrote articles in medical journals explaining why it was physically impossible for the human body to run a mile in less than four minutes.

However, in May 1954, a British medical student named Roger Bannister ran the mile in 3:59.4. His amazing accomplishment made headlines around the world. Yet what happened afterward is even more amazing. The four-minute mile was broken again the next month … and then again … and again. It has since been broken more than 700 times, sometimes by several people in the same race.

What happened? They weren't training any differently, but for the first time, they believed they could do it. The barriers to the mind had come down.

Never underestimate the power of belief when it comes to fulfilling your dreams. I can say with no hesitation that every person I've ever met who has achieved any degree of success has had one thing in common: They believed with all their hearts that they could do it.

You see, whether you think you can, or think you can't … you're right!

FAITH IS TAKING THE FIRST STEP EVEN WHEN
YOU DON'T SEE THE WHOLE STAIRCASE.

MARTIN LUTHER KING JR.

*K*eep your dreams alive. Understand to achieve anything
requires faith and belief in yourself, vision, hard work,
determination and dedication. Remember all things
are possible for those who believe.

GAIL DEVERS

TO ONE WHO HAS FAITH, NO EXPLANATION
IS NECESSARY. TO ONE WITHOUT FAITH,
NO EXPLANATION IS POSSIBLE.

SAINT THOMAS AQUINAS

FAITH IS A KNOWLEDGE WITHIN THE HEART,
BEYOND THE REACH OF PROOF.

KAHLIL GIBRAN

The only limit to our realization of tomorrow
will be our doubts of today. Let us move forward
with strong and active faith.

FRANKLIN D. ROOSEVELT

FAITH IS LIKE ELECTRICITY. YOU CAN'T SEE IT,
BUT YOU CAN SEE THE LIGHT.

UNKNOWN

*W*hen you have come to the edge of all light
that you know and are about to drop off into the
darkness of the unknown, faith is knowing one of
two things will happen: There will be something
solid to stand on or you will be taught to fly.

PATRICK OVERTON

FEED YOUR FAITH AND YOUR DOUBTS
WILL STARVE TO DEATH.

LES BROWN

*F*or I do not seek to understand in order to believe,
but I believe in order to understand.

SAINT ANSELM OF CANTERBURY

*F*aith goes up the stairs that love has built and
looks out the windows which hope has opened.

CHARLES H. SPURGEON

THEY CAN CONQUER WHO BELIEVE THEY CAN.

VIRGIL

*F*ear imprisons, faith liberates; fear paralyzes,
faith empowers; fear disheartens, faith encourages;
fear sickens, faith heals; fear makes useless,
faith makes serviceable.

HARRY EMERSON FOSDICK

WITHOUT FAITH, NOTHING IS POSSIBLE.
WITH IT, NOTHING IS IMPOSSIBLE.

MARY MCLEOD BETHUNE

Choose faith over doubt, choose faith over fear,
choose faith over the unknown and the unseen,
and choose faith over pessimism.

BISHOP RICHARD C. EDGLEY

FAITH IS TO BELIEVE WHAT YOU DO NOT SEE;
THE REWARD OF THIS FAITH IS
TO SEE WHAT YOU BELIEVE.

SAINT AUGUSTINE

"Love doesn't make the world go round.
Love is what makes the ride worthwhile."

FRANKLIN P. JONES

———— ◆ ————

LOVE IS POWERFUL. It can change everything in an instant…and for a lifetime. But, it's something that's not to be taken for granted. In fact, it's often the little things, the compliment, the extra hug, the special effort to make your loved one smile that makes love grow. This story shows that it's not the most expensive gift, but the gift of heart that makes the difference.

Love Not Expressed is Love Not Received
by Joanne Patek

My husband and I were married 30 years before he died suddenly from a heart attack. At that particular time in our lives, we were trying to pay cash for everything and get out of debt. His Datsun 280Z blew the engine and he was riding the bus to work while we saved for that repair.

Pat was an extraordinary man and a dedicated husband, father, son, friend and pastor to many. He would call me three times throughout the day and take the time to say, "I only have a fleeting moment and I wanted to give it to you, by saying how much I love you." On this one particular phone call, he was talking longer and lamenting with a whine, "How fast can we get the budget to move so that I can drive again?" he asked me.

After his call, I asked myself what fun thing I could do to show support and love for him in order to encourage and lift his spirits. I then proceeded to take my lunch, go to Walgreens, get a box of chalk and drive eight blocks from our house to where the bus left him off every day.

With that chalk, I drew big hearts on the street poles and sidewalk for all eight blocks and wrote the words, "Pat and Joanne Forever…True love to infinity and beyond…until the twelfth of never—forever I will be loving you."

On Pat's delightful walk home that evening, my LOVE was expressed all over for ALL to see, and it even stayed there for over a week for him to enjoy each evening as he emerged from the bus. I am so glad that I took the time to express myself so extravagantly, not knowing that he would die unexpectedly just a couple of months after that.

We never know when it is the last kiss or hug, so we try to never forget the power of each moment. Our family motto has always been, "Love not expressed is love not received." You can say you love me, but without expressing that love, I do not know it. I am so glad that I took the time to make that memory into a Kodak moment that day. What a lunch, and oh, what feeling it gave to both of us.

LOVE COMPLETES US.

PEGGY ANDERSON

THE LOVE WE GIVE AWAY IS
THE ONLY LOVE WE KEEP.

ELBERT HUBBARD

*P*ure love is a willingness to give
without a thought of receiving anything in return.

PEACE PILGRIM

LOVE IS JUST A WORD UNTIL SOMEONE COMES
ALONG AND GIVES IT MEANING.

PAULO COELHO

*L*ove is like the wind—
you can't see it, but you can feel it.

NICHOLAS SPARKS

LOVE IS TWO SOULS SHARING ONE DREAM.

MARY CRISORIO

*W*e cannot all do great things,
but we can do small things with great love.

MOTHER TERESA

I LOVE YOU, NOT ONLY FOR WHAT YOU ARE,
BUT FOR WHAT I AM WHEN I AM WITH YOU.

ELIZABETH BARRETT BROWNING

The best and most beautiful thing
in the world cannot be seen or even touched.
They must be felt with the heart.

HELEN KELLER

THROW YOUR HEART OVER THE FENCE
AND THE REST WILL FOLLOW.

NORMAN VINCENT PEALE

LOVE

COURAGE

"Courage doesn't always roar. Sometimes courage is the quiet voice at the end of the day saying, 'I will try again tomorrow.'"

MARY ANNE RADMACHER

———— • ◆ • ————

THIS BEAUTIFUL QUOTE by Mary Anne Radmacher was the inspiration for author Paula Fox's poem to women. Each of us faces obstacles every day. Paula shows us that it's the courage that we show in facing our challenges that gives us the strength to come out stronger on the other side:

Courage doesn't always roar…

By Paula Fox

When life gets you down and the problems you face
*   are certainly more than your share…*
When you run out of strength and you want to give up
*   because it's just too much to bear…*

I want to remind you, my precious friend,
*   that you have what it takes inside …*
extraordinary courage that may not ROAR
*   but it doesn't cower and hide.*

It's a quiet voice inside you that says,
  "Tomorrow I'll try again."
It's the courage to keep on going…
  to see things through to the end.

You are not defined by this moment in time.
  You are not what has happened to you.
It's the way that you choose to respond that matters
  and what you decide to do.

Courage is not the absence of fear,
  but a powerful choice we make.
It's the choice to move forward with PURPOSE and joy,
  regardless of what it takes.

It's the courage that's found in ordinary women
  who are HEROES in their own way…
exhibiting strength and fortitude
  in life's challenges every day…

For the WOMAN of COURAGE is a winner
    regardless of what she loses.
She displays amazing beauty and strength
    with the attitude she chooses.

She gives herself the permission she needs
    to feel disappointed or sad.
But then she empowers herself with FAITH…
    to focus on good things…not bad.

Her story is one of gentle strength
    reminding us all once more…
Steel is sometimes covered in velvet,
    and
Courage doesn't always roar!

*S*uccess is not final, failure is not fatal:
It is the courage to continue that counts.

WINSTON CHURCHILL

EFFORT ONLY FULLY RELEASES ITS REWARD
AFTER A PERSON REFUSES TO QUIT.

NAPOLEON HILL

A ship is safe in harbor but that's not what ships are for.

WILLIAM GREENOUGH THAYER SHEDD

A dream doesn't become reality through magic;
it takes sweat, determination and hard work.

COLIN POWELL

COURAGE IS GRACE UNDER PRESSURE.

ERNEST HEMINGWAY

*M*an cannot discover new oceans unless
he has the courage to lose sight of the shore.

ANDRÉ GIDE

NEVER CONFUSE A SINGLE DEFEAT WITH A FINAL DEFEAT.

F. SCOTT FITZGERALD

*W*hen there is no peril in the fight,
there is no glory in the triumph.

PIERRE CORNEILLE

ONE MAN WITH COURAGE MAKES A MAJORITY.

ANDREW JACKSON

*T*he difference between a successful person
and others is not a lack of strength, not a lack of knowledge,
but rather, a lack of will.

VINCE LOMBARDI JR.

COURAGE IS FEAR HOLDING ON
A MINUTE LONGER.

GENERAL GEORGE S. PATTON

*Y*ou may have to fight a battle more
than once to win it.

MARGARET THATCHER

THE BRICK WALLS ARE
THERE FOR A REASON.
THE BRICK WALLS ARE NOT
THERE TO KEEP US OUT.
THE BRICK WALLS ARE
THERE TO GIVE US A CHANCE TO SHOW
HOW BADLY WE WANT SOMETHING.
BECAUSE THE BRICK WALLS ARE
THERE TO STOP THE PEOPLE
WHO DON'T WANT IT BADLY ENOUGH.
THEY'RE THERE TO STOP THE OTHER PEOPLE.

RANDY PAUSCH

COURAGE

FAMILY

> *"… We start and end with family."*
>
> ANTHONY BRANDT

———— • ◆ • ————

OUR FAMILIES PROVIDE us with our roots…and our wings. At the end of your life, most of us wish we had spent less time at the office and more time with our families. Sometimes, those ordinary days are the ones that turn out to be the most treasured, as illustrated in this powerful story by best-selling author Lance Wubbels:

> *In the faint light of the attic, an old man, tall and stooped, bent his great frame and made his way to a stack of boxes that sat near one of the little half-windows. Brushing aside a wisp of cobwebs, he tilted the top box toward the light and began to carefully lift out one old photograph album after another. Eyes once bright but now dim searched longingly for the source that had drawn him here.*
>
> *It began with the fond recollection of the love of his life, long gone, and somewhere in these albums was a photo of her he hoped to rediscover. Silent as a mouse, he patiently opened the long-buried treasures and soon was lost in a sea of memories.*

Although his world had not stopped spinning when his wife left it, the past was more alive in his heart than his present aloneness.

Setting aside the dusty albums, he pulled from the box what appeared to be a journal from his grown son's childhood. He could not recall ever having seen it before, or that his son had ever kept a journal. Why did Elizabeth always save the children's old junk? he wondered, shaking his white head.

Opening the yellowed pages, he glanced over a short reading, and his lips curved in an unconscious smile. Even his eyes brightened as he read the words that spoke clear and sweet to his soul. It was the voice of the little boy who had grown up far too fast in this very house, and whose voice had grown fainter and fainter over the years. In the utter silence of the attic, the words of a guileless six-year-old worked their magic and carried the old man back to a time almost totally forgotten.

Entry after entry stirred a sentimental hunger in his heart like the longing a gardener feels in the winter for the fragrance of spring flowers. But it was accompanied by the painful memory that his son's simple recollections of those days were far different from his own. But how different?

Reminded that he had kept a daily journal of his business activities over the years, he closed his son's journal and turned to leave, having forgotten the cherished photo that originally triggered his search. Hunched over to keep from bumping his head on the rafters, the old man stepped to the wooden stairway and made his descent, then headed down a carpeted stairway that led to the den.

Opening a glass cabinet door, he reached in and pulled out an old business journal. Turning, he sat down at his desk and placed the two journals beside each other. His was leather-bound and engraved neatly with his name in gold, while his son's was tattered and the name "Jimmy" had been nearly scuffed from its surface. He ran a long, skinny finger over the letters, as though he could restore what had been worn away with time and use.

As he opened his journal, the old man's eyes fell upon an inscription that stood out because it was so brief in comparison to other days. In his own handwriting were these words:

Wasted the whole day fishing with Jimmy. Didn't catch a thing.

With a deep sigh and a shaking hand, he took Jimmy's journal and found the boy's entry for the same day, June 4. Large, scrawling letters pressed deeply into the paper read:

Went fishing with my dad. Best day of my life.

I know why families were created with
all their imperfections. They humanize you.
They are made to make you forget yourself occasionally,
so that the beautiful balance of life is not destroyed.

ANAÏS NIN

THE FAMILY IS THE SCHOOL OF DUTIES...
FOUNDED ON LOVE.

FELIX ADLER

*L*ove begins at home,
and it is not how much we do...
but how much love we put in that action.

MOTHER TERESA

IT IS NOT THE CARDS YOU HAVE BEEN DEALT,
BUT HOW YOU PLAY THEM THAT COUNTS.

B.L. ANDERSON

*F*eelings of worth can flourish only in an atmosphere
where individual differences are appreciated, mistakes are
tolerated, communication is open and rules are flexible—
the kind of atmosphere that is found in a nurturing family.

VIRGINIA SATIR

WHERE WE LOVE IS HOME—HOME THAT OUR
FEET MAY LEAVE, BUT NOT OUR HEARTS.

OLIVER WENDELL HOLMES

THE LIGHT IS WHAT GUIDES YOU HOME,
THE WARMTH IS WHAT KEEPS YOU THERE.

ELLIE RODRIGUEZ

———— • ◆ • ————

*Y*our family, and your love, must be cultivated
like a garden. Time, effort, and imagination
must be summoned constantly to keep any
relationship flourishing and growing.

JIM ROHN

FAMILY

*T*he only rock I know that stays steady,
the only institution I know that works, is the family.

LEE IACOCCA

THE FAMILY IS THE NUCLEUS OF CIVILIZATION.

WILL DURANT

A man travels the world over in search of what
he needs and returns home to find it.

GEORGE A. MOORE

IN EVERY CONCEIVABLE MANNER, THE FAMILY IS
A LINK TO OUR PAST, BRIDGE TO OUR FUTURE.

ALEX HALEY

It is around the family and the home that all the greatest virtues, the most dominating virtues of human society, are created, strengthened and maintained.

WINSTON CHURCHILL

*I*N FAMILY LIFE,

LOVE IS THE OIL THAT EASES FRICTION,

THE CEMENT THAT BINDS US CLOSER TOGETHER,

AND THE MUSIC THAT BRINGS HARMONY.

EVA BURROWS

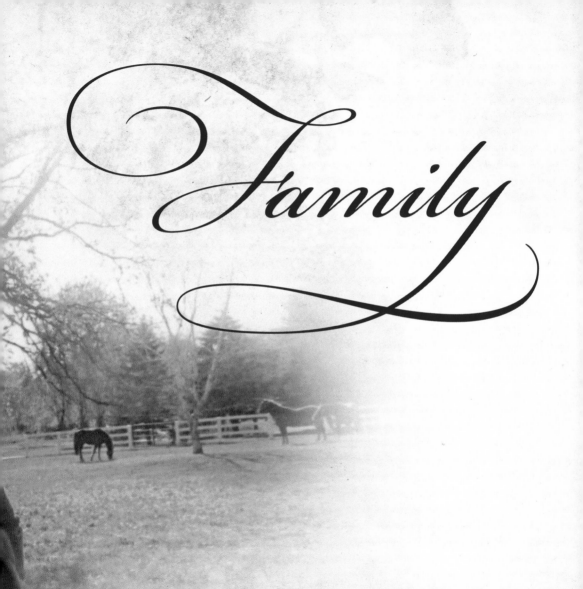

Family

FRIENDSHIP

"*A* friend is someone who knows
all about you and loves you just the same."

ELBERT HUBBARD

"Friendship doubles your joy and divides your grief."

SWEDISH PROVERB

FEW THINGS IN life are constant. Many things come and go, but having a lifelong friend is a treasure to be cherished. In her book, *Friends: The Family We Choose for Ourselves*, author and poet BJ Gallagher has just the right words to remind us that good friends are there to celebrate with us in good times and to listen and support us when times are tough:

That Which is Shareable is Bearable

BY BJ GALLAGHER

I've learned that
  if I can share my troubles
    I can bear them.

It's true.
It makes me feel better to have you around
    when I'm down.
Your presence reassures me;
    your listening soothes me;
      your hug consoles me.

It's nice to have company—
    even if it's in the pits.

I don't need cheery platitudes of positive thinking
    or booming bravado urging me to "buck up."

No...
    What I really need right now
    is just the comfort of your company ...

    and maybe a little chocolate.

*F*ate chooses your relations; you choose your friends.

JACQUES DELILLE

FRIENDSHIP DOUBLES OUR JOY
AND DIVIDES OUR GRIEF.

SWEDISH PROVERB

A friend is someone who knows the song in your heart,
and can sing it back to you when
you have forgotten the words.

BERNARD MELTZER

MY FRIENDS ARE MY ESTATE.

EMILY DICKINSON

*E*ach friend represents a world in us,
a world possibly not born until they arrive and
it is only by this meeting that a new world is born.

ANAÏS NIN

A SINGLE ROSE CAN BE MY GARDEN ...
A SINGLE FRIEND, MY WORLD.

LEO BUSCAGLIA

A FRIEND IS A PRESENT YOU GIVE YOURSELF.

ROBERT LOUIS STEVENSON

*P*eople will walk in and out of our lives,
but true friends will leave footprints on our hearts.

ELEANOR ROOSEVELT

FRIENDSHIP IS A SHELTERING TREE.

SAMUEL TAYLOR COLERIDGE

*W*hen the world is so complicated,
the simple gift of friendship
is within all of our hands.

MARIA SHRIVER

WHEN A FRIEND ASKS, THERE IS NO TOMORROW.

GEORGE HERBERT

*T*ruly great friends are hard to find,
difficult to leave and impossible to forget.

G. RANDOLF

A TRUE FRIEND REACHES FOR YOUR HAND
AND TOUCHES YOUR HEART.

HEATHER PRYOR

To be rich in friends is to be poor in nothing.

LILIAN WHITING

Friendship

HAPPINESS

"Most people are about as happy as they make up their minds to be."

ABRAHAM LINCOLN

I'VE LONG FELT the way Lincoln did. Happiness is a choice as much as anything—a choice of perception, a choice of attitude, a choice of how you respond to life, a choice of action.

In a great book, *Happiness Is a Choice*, by Barry Neil Kaufman, the author describes the experience he and his wife had with their third child, a baby boy who was diagnosed as autistic. At first, the couple was devastated.

However, once they worked through their initial reaction to the diagnosis, they made a life-altering decision: they chose to be happy. They said, "We can let this situation drag us into depression and self-pity, OR we can decide to love our child, make a nurturing family for him, and have a good life together. They chose the latter.

They rejected the advice of doctors who told them to put the child in an institution. Instead, they completely redesigned their home and their lives to meet the needs of their autistic toddler. He couldn't meet them in their world, so they met him in his.

Day by day, they were able to build rapport with their son, teach him new behaviors and caringly guide him to a more normal life. The boy grew and thrived under his parents' unconditional love, patience, and teaching—it was a long, challenging process, but he graduated from high school, then college, with honors. And throughout those challenging years, Barry Neil Kaufman and his wife chose happiness.

JOY IS NOT IN THINGS; IT IS IN US.

RICHARD WAGNER

*R*ules for happiness: something to do,
someone to love, something to hope for.

IMMANUEL KANT

THE HAPPINESS OF YOUR LIFE DEPENDS UPON THE QUALITY OF YOUR THOUGHTS...

MARCUS AURELIUS

*I*t was only a sunny smile and little it cost in the giving,
but like morning light it scattered the night
and made the day worth living.

F. SCOTT FITZGERALD

NONE BUT THOSE WHO ARE HAPPY
IN THEMSELVES CAN MAKE OTHERS SO.

ELIZA COOK

*T*he secret of happiness is not in doing what one likes,
but in liking what one does.

JAMES M. BARRIE

*F*or happiness one needs security,
but joy can spring like a flower even from the cliffs of despair.

ANNE MORROW LINDBERGH

BEAUTY IS WHATEVER GIVES JOY.

EDNA ST. VINCENT MILLAY

*O*ur brightest blazes of gladness are commonly
kindled by unexpected sparks.

SAMUEL JOHNSON

Happiness

THE HAPPIEST PEOPLE ARE THOSE
WHO DO THE MOST FOR OTHERS.

BOOKER T. WASHINGTON

*R*emember that happiness is a way of travel,
not a destination.

ROY GOODMAN

DON'T CRY BECAUSE IT'S OVER.
SMILE BECAUSE IT HAPPENED.

DR. SEUSS

HAPPINESS NEVER DECREASES
BY BEING SHARED.

BUDDHA

*S*uccess is not the key to happiness.
Happiness is the key to success.

ALBERT SCHWEITZER

SOME PURSUE HAPPINESS—OTHERS CREATE IT.

RALPH WALDO EMERSON

THE SUN DOES NOT SHINE FOR A
FEW TREES AND FLOWERS,
BUT FOR THE WIDE WORLD'S JOY.

HENRY WARD BEECHER

PURPOSE

"The purpose of life is a life of purpose."

ROBERT BYRNE

———— •✦• ————

WHAT ARE YOUR greatest gifts? How can you best serve mankind? These are questions you must answer to find your true purpose in life.

Who am I?

What am I meant to do here?

What am I trying to do with my life?

These are powerful questions that can be difficult to answer. They sometimes surface during major life transitions such as family strife, job loss, spiritual awakenings, or the death of a loved one.

Every person is a unique being. There is only one of you in the universe. You have many obvious gifts and other gifts still waiting to be discovered.

I truly believe, however, that one of the most important questions you can ask yourself in your journey to find your purpose is, "How can I serve others?"

Albert Schweitzer said it well: "I don't know what your destiny will be, but one thing I do know: the only ones among you who will be really happy are those who have sought and found how to serve."

*I*f you don't know where you're going,
any road will take you there.

LEWIS CARROLL

GREAT MINDS HAVE PURPOSES,
OTHERS HAVE WISHES.

WASHINGTON IRVING

*W*hen a man does not know what harbor
he is making for, no wind is the right wind.

LUCIUS ANNAEUS SENECA

*T*he way to get meaning into your life is to devote yourself to loving others, devote yourself to your community around you, and devote yourself to creating something that gives you purpose and meaning.

MITCH ALBOM

LIFE IS A REFLECTION OF INTENT.

JONATHAN LOCKWOOD HUIE

*I*t is a mistake to think that moving fast is the same as actually going somewhere.

STEVE GOODIER

YOU CANNOT BE LOST ON A ROAD
THAT IS STRAIGHT.

PROVERB

*A*ccept yourself, your strengths,
your weaknesses, your truths,
and know what tools you have to fulfill your purpose.

STEVE MARABOLI

PUR

*S*trong lives are motivated by dynamic purposes;
lesser ones exist on wishes and inclinations.

KENNETH HILDEBRAND

THE BEST WAY TO PREDICT
YOUR FUTURE IS TO CREATE IT.

ABRAHAM LINCOLN

*T*he meaning of life is to find your gift;
the purpose of life is to give it away.

PABLO PICASSO

*T*wenty years from now you will be
more disappointed by the things you didn't do
than by the ones you did. So throw off the bowlines,
sail away from the safe harbor. Catch the trade winds
in your sails. Explore. Dream. Discover.

MARK TWAIN

TO REACH A PORT, WE MUST SAIL—
SAIL, NOT TIE AT ANCHOR—
SAIL, NOT DRIFT.

FRANKLIN D. ROOSEVELT

*F*ind what makes your heart sing,
and create your own music in life.

MAC ANDERSON

*I*f one advances confidently in the direction
of his dreams … he will meet with a success
unexpected in common hours.

HENRY DAVID THOREAU

EFFORT AND COURAGE ARE NOT ENOUGH
WITHOUT PURPOSE AND DIRECTION.

JOHN F. KENNEDY

*T*he purpose of our lives is to give
birth to the best which is within us.

MARIANNE WILLIAMSON

CONCLUSION

FOR ME, QUOTATIONS capture the best thoughts of some of the world's greatest thinkers in a way that opens the mind to new insights. Long after you turn the last page, I hope that this book of stories and quotations continues to be a source of inspiration for you.

It is real values—*gratitude, character, kindness, faith, love, courage, family, friendship, happiness and purpose*—that help us to remember…

"THE BEST THINGS IN LIFE AREN'T THINGS."

Peggy Anderson

PEGGY ANDERSON

ABOUT THE AUTHOR

Over the past twenty years, Peggy Anderson has compiled more than one dozen quotation books on various topics. Her books have sold more than 600,000 copies.

THE BEST *things* IN *life* AREN'T THINGS

Cover and internal design © 2013 by Simple Truths.
Simple Truths is a registered trademark.

Published by Simple Truths, an imprint of Sourcebooks, Inc.
P.O. Box 4410, Naperville, Illinois 60567-4410
(630) 961-3900 • Fax: (630) 961-2168

www.sourcebooks.com

Design and production: Lynn Harker
Edited by: Alice Patenaude

All images provide by Thinkstock and Shutterstock.

Simple Truths is a registered trademark.
Printed and bound in the United States of America

ISBN 978-1-60810-248-8

01 WOZ 13

If you have enjoyed this book we invite you to check out our entire collection of gift books, with free inspirational movies, at **www.simpletruths.com.** You'll discover it's a great way to inspire *friends* and *family*, or to thank your best *customers* and *employees*.

For more information, please visit us at:

www.simpletruths.com

Or call us toll free... **800-900-3427**